No part of this publication may be reproduced in whole or in part, or stored, or transmitted in any form without written permission of the author.

For information regarding permission, please email the author, Jonathan Cutillo, at jonathan@eastamericanedu.com.

New Old-Fashioned Riddles is a publication of East American Education LLC.

All rights reserved.

Introduction

Dear Reader,

You will find a riddle on the front of each page. The author recommends reading the riddle out loud and letting everyone around have time to answer it before turning the page. On the back, you will find the answer along with some tidbits of information regarding the answer. Let everyone have a chance before you peek!

To get the most out of this book, take your time going through it. Some of the riddles you might get right away. Others are more difficult. They are not in any particular order. Try a riddle or two each day along with your friends or family.

Enjoy the riddles and the information provided. I hope they lead to some good discussions, and most of all I hope the book is fun for all of the thinkers around you, great and small.

Sincerely,

        Jonathan Cutillo

Little green hats on little red faces

arrive in June and take their places

Hiding out among the grasses

until they're found by lads and lasses

Strawberries

Strawberries, which could as well be called "grass berries," generally yield their fruit in June. Some species will yield a second crop in late summer.

As their name suggests, they often grow among the grasses on leafy low-lying stalks. Unless the strawberry patch is kept free of grasses and other intruders, one must search carefully for these delicious fruits. Once you taste a strawberry ripe from the garden or field, you won't mind having to search for another one.

She frolics in the heather

and flies without a feather

Stores up her golden treasure

to weather winter weather

Honey-bee

Honey-bees, like most insects, have wings to fly but no feathers. Bees travel from flower to flower to collect pollen. When the heather is in bloom, they could be said to "frolic in the heather." Bees carry pollen in small sacks behind their rear legs. They take it back to the hive, where they make and store honey. The stored honey is the bees' winter food source, and beekeepers know better than to collect honey too late in the summer.

It is the female worker bees who do most of the work of the hive, including foraging for pollen and nectar. The male bees, or drones, have more limited responsibilities. They are kicked out of the hive in the winter.

Old Jack Spanner has a back that is bent

and feet that are firmly stuck in cement

Though at his side daydreamers tarry

there's never been a load he couldn't carry

Bridge

The distance that a bridge traverses between its footings is known as the span. Both stone arch bridges and many modern bridges have shapes that resemble the bending of a back. Moreover, bridges are always built on solid footings, hence his feet being firmly stuck in cement.

"At his side daydreamers tarry" refers to an image common to our imagination.

Finally, bridges are said to carry the weight of loads that cross them. If a load too heavy for the structure of the bridge were brought across, it would fail. Fortunately, this seldom ever happens.

Who has a head of gold

and then a head of grey

That fellow's as bald as can be

after a windy day

Dandelion

When dandelions first bloom, they speckle the lawn with bright, golden flowers. After a few days, however, the yellow fades into whitish-grey seed parachutes. Children often enjoy picking the white dandelions and blowing the seeds off of them. But if they don't, the wind will do the job for them. The parachutes are carried by the wind whither it will, and this is how dandelions spread. All that is left is the bald head of the stalk.

Many caretakers of lawns look upon them as weeds. Even so, dandelions do not only produce pretty flowers, they are also almost completely edible. The flowers and greens can be eaten, and the roots make an excellent detoxifying tea.

Willy Wispy has more than one hue

all decked in white and purple and blue

In a dark mood he wept and cried

and all the children ran inside

Cloud

Although we often think of clouds as being white, really they are bedecked with many hues, often purples and blues. Is there really such thing as pure white in nature? At the extremes of the day, they are even more colorful, a sight to behold.

At times clouds are wispy, especially cirrus clouds. At times there are large puffy cumulous clouds. Different types of clouds form at different altitudes. But when the sky is filled with dark clouds, rain is usually on the way. When the clouds weep, children run inside.

Entirely metal

except for the seat

and the places I put

my hands and my feet

and where it should happen

to touch the ground

where it goes round

and round and round

Bicycle

Bicycles are constructed of a metal frame, handlebars, sprocket, and chain. Traditionally, bikes were made of steel. Modern bicycles are often made from aluminum, which makes them much lighter. Therefore, bikes are entirely metal, almost.

The seat of a bicycle is padded and wrapped in leather, or a similar synthetic material. Pedals, especially on children's bikes, are often made of plastic. Finally, the hand grips and tires are made of rubber.

What make the leaves of Autumn

such a pretty sight

All together they're black

None are white

Pigments

Pigments are the compounds that give things their color. Pigments absorb and reflect certain lights, and the ones reflected are the ones that we see. During the summer, everything is so green. That is because chlorophyl, the chemical that helps plants to absorb sunlight for photosynthesis, is green. As the weather cools and the days shorten, plants stop the process of photosynthesis and the chlorophyl in the leaves breaks down. What is left over are the other pigments that reside in the leaves, which we enjoy every autumn.

There are three primary pigments: magenta, cyan, and yellow. From these colors, you can mix any color you want. If you mix them all, you will get black. If you don't use any, you will have white.

As many strings as a seamstress

As many hammers as a hardware store

As many keys as a castle

All locked behind one door

Piano

The piano, like many musical instruments, produces its sound from the vibration of strings. What makes a piano different from most other stringed instruments is that the strings are neither plucked nor bowed. Rather, each set of strings is struck by a hammer, making the piano both a percussion instrument and a stringed instrument.

The piano in my home has two hundred and twenty-five strings. They are struck by eighty-eight hammers, each of which is set in motion by its own key. All the keys can be locked behind the fallboard, the hinged piece of wood that you can open and close like a door.

Who cooks for you

when he's in a talkative mood

His appetite is good

but he can't keep down his food

Owl

All owls are well known for saying "who." But the Barred Owl has an entire sentence to say, "Who cooks for you?" So when he is in a talkative mood, you will hear this sentence.

Like all birds of prey, owls consume small animals and then regurgitate pellets containing the indigestible portions of the animal. Often in elementary science classes, students will dissect these pellets and try to identify the unfortunate creature that was the owl's meal.

What has leaves in number like a tree

and speaks to me but silently

If I willed it would be heard

I'd lend my voice to every word

Book

Pages of a book are also referred to as leaves. You may know the saying, "Turn over a new leaf." That means to make a change that will alter your attitude or behavior. And of course "loose-leaf paper" refers to paper that is not bound.

Books, like the one you are reading now, do not make any noise of their own. But they do speak to us by their printed words and images. When we read aloud, we lend the book our voice as we make what is written audible for those around us.

High and low in noblemen's castles

and teaching arithmetic to rascals

Hard as bone and flat as paper

It can only be procured in nature

Slate

Slate is both flat and durable. Because of these qualities it has been used for roofing and flooring. Although it is rather expensive, it is both beautiful and very long lasting. Those who can afford it still sometimes use it for these purposes, be they noblemen or not.

Another time-honored tradition that has long faded is the use of slate as a chalkboard. Students in schools once had their very own "slates" that they would use to practice writing and arithmetic. These archaic tablets have, for better or worse, given way first to notebooks and then to computerized tablets in most academic settings.

Thriving on a rainy day

among the things that decay

Has not root nor leaf nor seed

yet it grows fast as a weed

Mushrooms

If you take a walk through the woods on a warm and damp day, you will be almost certain to see some mushrooms. They grow in areas where there is not an abundance of sunlight, often on decaying wood and other organic material.

Mushrooms are not plants. They are fungi. They do not have roots, leaves, or seeds. They do not need sunlight to live. They procreate by spreading spores that in the right conditions will grow into new mushrooms. They have root-like appendages called mycelium that help the organism to absorb moisture and other nutrients. Even so, being a fungi means having no roots.

What often has wheels

Never has wings

Travels by air, land and sea

Enclosing every thing

Suitcase

Long gone are the days when travelers had to carry heavy suitcases. Most modern suitcases are equipped with wheels and a telescoping handle that make them very easy to move without doing any heavy lifting. They don't, however, have wings.

If you like to travel, whether by air, land, or sea, you are surely well acquainted with a suitcase or two. In it you can enclose everything you would like to bring with you on your travels. Bon Voyage!

A sound that delights

or one that bothers

depending on how it's placed

among its sisters and its brothers

Musical Note

If you have ever learned to play an instrument, or have been around someone who was learning, you surely know how bad it can sound when a wrong note is played. Conversely, it is delightful to hear each correct note in a sequence. But what makes a note the wrong note? Why do some notes sound so lovely, some so terrible, some so happy, and some so sad?

Musical notes are at intervals from other musical notes. How a particular note sounds at a given place in a progression of notes depends on the other notes that come before and after the note. For an easy demonstration of this, try the familiar melody in the illustration. For a more detailed explanation, please ask your music teacher.

Red as rust

Hard as stone

Put them in a row

and call it Home

Bricks

Bricks have been used in construction for thousands of years. They are made of clay, and generally baked in an oven until they are dry and hard. Bricklayers typically use mortar, a mixture of Portland cement, sand, and lime, to adhere the bricks to one another.

In some areas, bricks have become less common as a primary construction material. But they are still often used as a facade over wooden construction. If only the front of a home is made of brick, it is likely a facade. However, if the entire home seems to be made of brick, it most likely is actually constructed of brick.

Timid Tom never leaves his house

Some think he's lazy as a louse

But he never sits down

nor lays on his back

And he swims quite well

as a matter of fact

Turtle

Turtles are relatively slow movers on land. It makes them seem lazy, and perhaps they are. Seldom do you see a turtle running. It will not run away from you. But it might go inside its house and wait for you to go away.

Turtles are excellent swimmers. Even turtles you see slowly foraging on land are quite at home in the water. Some turtles, like the Green Sea Turtle, spend almost all of their lives in the water. But even turtles who live in the water cannot breath under water. They are reptiles, not fish. Turtles that are not adept swimmers are usually referred to as tortoises.

Patty is covered all over with scales

She and her sisters hang from their tails

Children are glad when they can be found

And with sticky fingers pull them down

Pinecones

The scaly pinecones that you easily observe hanging from a tree are the females. The male cones are much harder to spot and are less wood-like. The cones are said to be female because they produce the seed, which must be pollenated by the male cone in order to produce a new pine tree.

If you research the etymology of the word cone, you will find that it comes from the Greek word "konus," which actually means "pinecone." Pine trees are conifers, trees that produce seed-containing cones. You can see the word cone without the e on the end at the beginning of conifer. An easy way to remember what conifer means, is to make a note of this. It is a "cone-ifer."

Twin faces with vertical eyes

donned expressions of surprise

Frightened I struck one carelessly

and was filled with negative energy

If these faces you happen to see

be as careful as you can be

Electrical Outlet

If you live in the North American continent, Taiwan, Japan, parts of South America, or the Caribbean, you probably got this riddle. Many other parts of the world use outlets that do not resemble twin faces with vertical eyes.

Electricity gets its name from electrons, negatively charged sub-atomic particles. In electrical generation, these negatively charged particles are set free and set in motion to either move around a circuit (DC) or to bounce into one other in alternating movement (AC).

While that is all complicated, we do know to be careful around electrical outlets.

Trodden by sparrows

resting their wings

Adorns peasants' houses

Stands above kings

Roof

Every abode has a roof, from the most extravagant of palaces down to the most humble of cottages. A roof is both a vital and aesthetic part of the house. As an aesthetic element, it adorns a house.

The house sparrow is often perched on the roof of a house. That is because house sparrows usually live in the eaves or walls of buildings, or other man-made structures. They are relatively unafraid of people and prefer to live in developed locations to the wild. Look for some where you live.

What is black as night

and floats on a sea of white

It tells a story

but makes no sound

It helps the news

to get around

Ink

Ink is often black. Paper is the sea of white on which it floats.

Long before the days of the screen, men used ink to express their thoughts in written language. Before the printing press, each and every book had to be written by hand. Once movable type appeared, the mass dissemination of ideas, good and bad, was made possible. Books became affordable for the masses. Newspapers shook the foundations of the world. And it was all done with ink. The pen is mightier than the sword.

What seat is above all others

the prince of which is richly served

Yet when he gains stature

he'll be lowered as he deserves

Highchair

Very small children are not entirely able to manage their own cups and cutlery. Those around them, quite often their mothers, help them to get on with their meals. As they grow, they become increasingly self-sufficient. When the day comes where they have grown enough to sit in big-boy chairs, out of their high places they go. From then on they sit down low with the rest of us, and they probably deserve it.

But while they're small, the little princes and princesses can sit up high while those around them serve them to their heart's content.

It can keep you alive

It can make you dead

It can be blue

It can be red

Enough is a word

It never has said

Fire

In Greek mythology, the Titan Prometheus with the help of Athena, the goddess of wisdom, stole fire from heaven and gave it to man. That placed man in a position greater than all other animals. It also allowed him to cook his food and warm his home. Later the gods punished Prometheus for he had made man equal to the gods.

According to the proverbs of Solomon, fire never is satisfied. If you have ever sat around a fire, you know that sticks and logs must continuously be added to the fire to keep it going. The more fuel that you add to the fire, the more it will consume. It never says "enough."

Soft in the ground

and hard on the table

Make it into any shape

that you are able

Clay

Clay is a broad term for several clay minerals and often the impurities that help to give them their colors. More pure mixes of clay are white or grey. Less pure mixes can even tend to be mud-colored, and at a certain point the mix is no longer known as clay, but as loam. Loam is a mixture of clay and soil that was used for building in ancient times.

If you live in an area with high clay content in the soil, it may be possible to find some pure clay deposits. If ever you are digging and start to unearth grayish, dense, and moldable material, it is likely clay. High quality clay can also be purchased. Shape it however you can and bake it.

His body is slender

He has three feet

On his wide flat head

he wears a sheet

He's there when I play

a melody sweet

I can fold him up

so nice and neat

Music Stand

If you study a musical instrument other than a keyboard, you probably have a music stand that you use. Most pianos and other keyboard instruments have an integrated music stand that does not require its own support. Generally, music stands consist of a tripod topped by a wide, flat, angled head on which sheet music is placed.

Portability is often a consideration, as both amateur and professional musicians do not always play music at a single location. Therefore, many music stands can be folded up nicely and neatly, placed in a tote bag, and taken with you to your next performance or lesson.

Three black whiskers

on a white face

Regardless of the weather

they wouldn't stay together

but each went about

at its own pace

Clock

Time sometimes does seem to move slowly, and sometimes it seems to move very quickly. If you are outside playing with your friends on a sunny summer day, the hours roll by without a thought to the time. On the other hand, if you are stuck inside without a good book to read while it is cold and rainy, you may find yourself counting the minutes in the hour.

But time is not subject to our perceptions. The three black whiskers on the face of the clock each move about at a steady pace, regardless of the weather or anything else.

Holds the earth

Counts in rings

Has arms but no face

Stays in one place

Tree

You can count the years of a tree's life by examining a cut section of the trunk. If a tree has been cut down near your house, examine the stump. You will see several rings of light and dark wood. These correspond to the yearly growth cycle of the tree. These seasonal growth rings are especially apparent wherever the weather changes seasonally, and less so in tropical environments.

Like all plants, trees hold the earth with their roots. This is vital for the life of the tree, and also very helpful to the landscape as a protection against erosion from wind and rain. Trees have branches like arms. They do not have faces, although sometimes scars on a tree's bark may resemble one.

Sleeps for a thousand years

yet in a single day

covers mile upon mile

with darkness and dismay

Volcano

The first thing one usually associates with a volcano is rivers of lava flowing out of the bowels of the earth. Entire mountains and islands have been formed from the flow of molten rock. However, it is the ash cloud that has the farthest reaching effect of an erupting volcano. In some of the world's most infamous volcanic eruptions, the ash covered areas of tens of thousands of square miles, with devastating effects.

Volcanos that are apparently inactive are known as dormant volcanoes. If you are familiar with any Latin languages, you probably know that dormant means sleeping. Volcanos may remain dormant for thousands of years, and yet they may one day again erupt, causing darkness and dismay.

I held a piece of ice

that wasn't cold

Found a lovely crystal

that wasn't old

I beheld a rainbow

that wasn't in the sky

Tell me what it is

and do not lie

Prism

Sometimes after a rainfall, the moisture droplets still present in the air refract the light of the sun. The wavelengths of the various colors of light reflect at different angles, and the effect is the entire spectrum of colors of light. Likewise, when light passes through a prism, the different wavelengths bend at different angles and a rainbow is formed.

White light contains all of the colors of the rainbow. When it is separated, the colors of the rainbow appear. Conversely, if you shined individually colored lights all together, the result would be white. Light theory works in reverse of pigment theory. Look back at the pigment description for a comparison. Lights and pigments work together to create our beautiful visual world.

Soundless billows

Formless dances

Wingless rises

Footless prances

Spreading around

'til it can't be found

Smoke

Smoke is often thick and apparent when it billows out of a chimney or smokestack. It rises up into the air. As it goes on its way, it dances and prances across the rooftops or tree tops. As it moves away from the chimney or smokestack, the smoke spreads out into the air. It becomes more and more transparent until it has vanished completely. It can no longer be found.

Shaped like a shoe

Moved by hand

Carries four feet

Not on land

Canoe

Canoes are open vessels that are long, thin and pointed at both ends. They especially resemble the fashionable shoes of the Ottoman Empire. Most canoes are designed to carry two passengers, but other arrangements do exist. The most notable are singe-passenger vessels. In the UK, the term canoe also includes boats that are closed on top, which are elsewhere known as kayaks.

Canoes are usually propelled by paddles, which unlike the oars of a rowboat are not connected to the craft. They are held and guided by the hands of the passengers. If there are two passengers, the canoes do indeed carry four feet. Never, however, on dry land.

In weather fair

My ribs I cup

In weather foul

I put them up

Umbrella

When an umbrella is folded, the tips of the ribs are placed in the tip cup. When an umbrella is opened, the ribs go up and give structure to the canopy.

There is a certain sort of umbrella that is used in fair weather to offer some protection from the sun. It is known as a parasol, meaning "sunshield." However, in places where it is still fashionable to keep the sun off, mostly in Asia, often the same umbrella is now used in good and bad weather. In most western countries, on the other hand, it has become more fashionable to get a suntan. Therefore, the ribs are cupped in weather fair.

'Tis the work of one's hands

Hangs as high as one's head

Tells of a place at a time

though never a word be said

Painting

In a world where almost any moment in place and in time can be very easily captured by the magical art known as digital photography, it is a wonder that paintings continue to capture our attention and inspire our imaginations. Yet they do, and that is why we still hang them, at eye-level of course, on the walls of our rooms.

There is some magic in an artists touch, in the deception and imperfection of his work, that shows us that particular place at that particular time in a different light. It is the work of the artist's hand, and therein lies the beauty.

Seeks the lowest place

Secretly raised up high

Adorns the blue with lace

Descends by and by

Water

In the Dao De Jing, Lao Tsu likens the highest good to water, for "water seeks the lowest place." The Lord Jesus likewise teaches man to seek the lowest place. "He who exalts himself will be humbled; he who humbles himself will be exalted."

Water is also exalted to high places, though we do not perceive it being lifted to the heavens. It condenses to paint the blue sky with clouds like lace. Afterwards, water descends to the earth and continues its course downward to the sea.

Made in the USA
Columbia, SC
22 October 2024